Legal Notice

Disclaimer Notice

MATH RIDDLES FOR KIDS (THE CONTINENT EDITION)

VOL 1

FOR KIDS 6-12 YEARS OLD with interactive math questions around the 7 continents of the world! You have purchased Volume 1, which consists of the first 4 continents, while Volume 2 consists of the remaining 3 continents.

INTRODUCTION

Dear Parents,

Would you like to get your hands on a book that not only polishes your child's problem-solving skills in mathematics but also boosts their knowledge of world geography?

If you have a hard time getting your child to read books and you can't engage them in solving math problems in a workbook or a worksheet, as is the case in traditional school books, then this book is your solution.

If you have not purchased the audible version of this book, I highly recommend it, as your child will likely feel like having a personal teacher narrate questions and wait for an answer before responding.

Audiobook learning has proven to be a fun and interactive experience for children.

Alternatively, you can join in with your little ones at home, on the go, or any time in between for a learning experience everyone will love.

Some questions you will assist them with, some you might find challenging yourself, but most importantly, it will be an excellent opportunity for family time.

Math riddles are a great way to evolve children's problem-solving skills, and it helps to cultivate their love for math. It engages them fully in tricky and interesting challenges while fostering a love for the subject.

Moreover, studies have shown that this adopted methodology for math learning improves arithmetic and pattern recognition. The unique riddles customized to each continent will also improve rational thinking and flex their brain muscles.

This first volume of the continent edition of math riddles for kids by Maisy Miller is for children aged 6-12 years old. It allows your child to travel around the world while solving fun riddles at the same time. This book is primarily designed to help your child level up their math skills while making it an exciting learning experience while gaining valuable information regarding the geography around the globe.

Now don't worry about the learning loss in summer schools, school breaks, or school cancellations. If your child is alienated by the traditional old-school methods that make learning more like a burden and a dreading task, this book is going to bridge the gap between learning and recreation.

Like 7 continents around the world, Vol 1 and Vol 2 will have 7 chapters that have riddles starting from the basic level in the first continent and progressing to harder ones as they go through the chapters.

These riddles will further enhance their knowledge about countries, oceans, and famous places in each continent. These riddles are based on real-life places and monuments around the world.

I have also included some math-related brain twisters in between the math riddles to make the pace interesting. It also helps engage the kids with some unconventional ways of thinking – so-called "Thinking Outside The Box". When established correctly, a strong foundation of mathematical skills supports children throughout their life.

By the end of this book, your child will not only be able to solve advanced-level riddles, but they will have acquired the knowledge of different continents and their respective places in a more memorable way.

I have given small answers to some questions, and I have provided answers with explanations to others. That way, it gives your child a better understanding of proceeding with those types of questions.

So, let's start our journey!

CH 1: WELCOME TO NORTH AMERICA!

It is the third-largest and fourth-most populous continent in the world. It is surrounded by the Pacific and Atlantic oceans. This continent has the world's second and third largest countries by area, Canada and the United States of America, respectively.

It has 23 countries. Greenland, which is the biggest island in the world, is also part of this continent.
It is the only continent in the world that has all types of climates in it. The widely spoken languages in this continent are English and Spanish. It is one of the most developed economic regions of the world.

We have some simple math riddles in this section to warm you up. Let's get to it.

No Cheating, but the answers are at the end of each chapter.

1. If it rains at midnight at the statue of liberty in New York, USA after 48 hours, will the sunshine be seen?

2. The Grand Canyon in Arizona, USA has two sacks. Which one is heavier? One pound of rocks or one pound of feathers?

3. There are 12 seashells and 6 stones at Cancun Beach in Mexico. What is the total of seashells and stones?

4. Sally went to Hawaii volcanoes national park. She saw five girls on her way. Every girl had two babies with her and each baby had five beads on their neck. How many persons were going to Hawaii volcanoes national park in total?

5. Adam was going to Costa Rica with his friends. He had 6 candies with him. He gave 2 candies to each of his friends. How many friends does he have?

6. I visited Washington DC, in the USA in a month that has 28 days. Which month is it?

7. You went with John on a picnic at Niagara Falls, Ontario, Canada. John brought 7 oranges in a bag. You took four from it. How many oranges do you have?

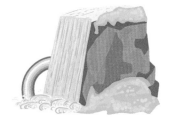

8. I lost my number friend at Toronto's CN Tower in Canada. Help me to find it. It is an odd number. But if you snatch an alphabet from it, it becomes even. What is it?

9. In the Gulf of Mexico, a math book told something to another math book. Guess what it was?

10. Lily's mother lives in Cuba. She has 3 children. Zara, flip, and ___?

11. A yellow leaf is 9 inches long and a blue leaf is 5 inches long in Yosemite National Park in California, USA. Which leaf is longer than the other?

12. Sara was standing in a queue at her school in Panama. There were 3 girls in front of her and 2 boys behind her. How many children are there in the queue?

Are you doing good so far? Wow, that's great. If not, then no worries. We have lots more to turn you into a champ. Let's keep practicing!

13. There is someone in Guatemala that has a face and hands, but it can't smile or hold anything. Can you tell me what is it?

14. A banana went to a beach party on Bahamas Island. It met 5 apples and 3 coconuts there. Can you tell how many fruits the banana met on the island?

15. Jack was going to Cuba. He had 9 balls with him. He lost 4 on the way. How many balls were left?

16. What does a math teacher like to eat in The Bahamas?

17. Gary goes on vacation to Mexico for 5 days. He spends the same number of days in the USA. What are the total days of his vacation?

18. A number lives in Jamaica; it is between 1 and 5. It is less than 4 and more than 2. Which number is it?

19. Martha is going to Disneyland Park in California, USA. She saw 5 princesses and 4 other characters there. Can you tell the total number of princesses and characters she saw there?

20. Lucy is measuring the length of a rock at the Grand Canyon, USA. Her measuring tape is only 6 inches long. It took her 2 lengths of measuring tape to measure the rock. What is the length of the rock?

21. Sam lives on Barbados Island. If he has 3 yellow sticks and 7 red sticks. How many sticks does he have altogether?

22. Parliament Hill in Ottawa, Canada is holding a festival for Easter. Bob dyes 3 eggs and Joan dyes 13 eggs. How many dyed Easter eggs do the boys have now?

23. Mr. White ate 2 doughnuts every day in Washington DC in the USA for 6 days. What is the total number of doughnuts that he ate in 6 days?

24. There is a historic one-story house in old Montreal in Canada. Everything is red inside. Red furniture, red walls, red carpet. What is the color of the stairs?

25. Maria, Sam, and Wendy had a party at Times Square in New York, USA. Everyone brought 4 sandwiches for the party. How many sandwiches do they have in total?

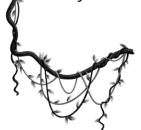

26. Allen camped for 2 hours at the Gabon rainforest in El Salvador. Steve camped for half of Allen's time. How much time did Steve spend in the rainforest?

27. A fish is 13 meters long in the Dominican Republic. Another fish is 2 meters shorter than the first one. What is the length of the second fish?

28. It's Brad's birthday today. He is celebrating it in Copper Canyon in Mexico. You can find his age if you add 3 to 10. How old is Brad?

29. Andy is making bread that requires 3 cups of flour. If he wants to make 2 loaves of bread, how many cups of flour will he need?

30. Harry played ice hockey daily for a week in Canada. How many times did he play Ice Hockey?

31. Lucy had an older bill of fifty and Flip had a newer one. Which bill is worth more than the other?

32. Tess is researching trees in Banff National Park in Alberta, Canada. One tree is 20 feet tall, and another is 10 feet tall. What is the difference in their height?

33. There are 6 Cherries on a tree at the Bay of Fundy in Canada. A bird eats 2 of them. How many are left behind on the tree?

34. The "Legoland" in the United States of America has 5 old fun rides and 4 new rides. How many total rides are there now?

Bravo, little friends!

It seems you are done with the simple Math riddles in North America, and you are now acquainted well with this continent.

Let's go to our next destination.

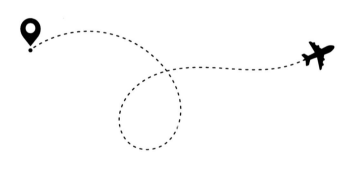

ANSWERS TO CHAPTER 1
QUESTIONS 1-34

1. No, sunshine can't be seen after 48 hours as it will be midnight again.
2. Neither. They both are the same being weighed one ton each.
3. There are a total of 18 seashells and stones.
4. Only Sally was going to Hawaii volcanoes national park.
5. Adam has 3 friends.
6. Well! All 12 months of a year have 28 days. ☺
7. You have four oranges. I told you!
8. It's Seven
9. I have lots of problems.
10. Oh yeah! It's Lily of course.
11. The yellow leaf is longer than the blue leaf.
12. There are 6 children. If you said 5, you forgot to include Sara!
13. Tick tock tick. You are right. It's a clock
14. The banana met 8 fruits. 5 plus 3 equals 8.
15. 5 balls
16. A Pi (e)
17. Gary's total days of vacation are 10 days. 5 days in Mexico and 5 days in the USA which altogether makes it 10.
18. Number 3
19. She saw 9 characters and princesses.
20. The rock is 12 inches long as 2 times 6 is 12.
21. The total number of sticks is 10
22. They have 16 eggs.
23. He ate 12 doughnuts. OH! That is a lot of sugar!
24. No stairs. Remember, it's a one-story house.
25. They have 12 sandwiches, 4 multiplied with 3 is12.
26. Steve camped for 1 hour because half of 2 is 1.
27. The second fish is 11 meters long.
28. Brad turned 13. Happy birthday Brad!
29. He will need 6 cups of flour to make 2 loaves of bread.
30. He played ice hockey 7 times because there are 7 days a week.
31. $50 bill has more worth than $1 bill (a newer one).
32. The difference is 10 feet.
33. 4 Cherries are left behind
34. 9 rides

CH 2: OLA AMIGOS!
WELCOME TO SOUTH AMERICA!

South America is divided into 12 countries, but hundreds of languages are spoken here. It is bound by the Pacific Ocean and the Atlantic Ocean. It has the world's largest Andes Mountain Range and the world's second-largest Amazon River.

The Amazon Rainforest provides 6% of the earth's oxygen and is one of the most important natural resources.

It's time to step up from Easy math riddles while exploring different countries and places in South America.

35. Twenty people are invited to the Samba party in Rio de Janeiro in Brazil. Seven people did not come to the party. How many people attended the party?

36. Some toads were sitting on a log in Galapagos Island, Ecuador. After 3 of them jumped in the water, there were 6 frogs left on the log. How many frogs were there in the beginning?

37. The Maua square in Brazil is a perfect square. How many corners does a square have?

38. Harry goes to the gym daily in French Guiana. After 2 weeks, how many days did harry go in total?

39. There are 12 students in Latin class and 3 students in English class in a language school in Peru. How many students are there altogether?

40. The Angel Falls in Venezuela is the world's highest waterfall. Imagine if it is 10 meters high and another waterfall is 2 meters shorter than it. What is the height of the second waterfall?

41. In Argentina, the children go to school at 8:00 am and return home at 10:00 am. For how many hours do the children stay at school?

42. Three girls went to a party in El Salvador that was the first capital of Brazil. Each girl had 10 boxes of juices. How many boxes of juice were there in total?

43. Stacy goes on a vacation to the Marble caves in Chile. She collects 18 blue marbles and 5 white marbles. How many marbles did she collect in total?

44. The Mindo valley in Ecuador has 2 mountains. First Mountain is 30KM high, and the second one is 40 KM high. What is the difference between the two mountains?

45. The Iguazu Falls lie between Brazil and Argentina. If Argentina has 30 KMs of the falls area and Brazil has an area that is half of it. What is the area of falls in Brazil?

46. Twenty-five birds were sitting on a tree in Easter Island, Chile. Some more birds came to join them. Then there were 30 birds on the tree. How many birds flew up to the tree?

47. I saw 2 cats and 1 dog in Buenos Aires in Argentina. How many legs did I see?

48. The shape of the Atacama Desert in Chile is an interesting one with 2 short sides and 2 long sides. What is the shape of the desert?

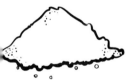

49. The largest salt flat in the world is Salar de Uyuni in Bolivia. Suppose Billy takes 9 grams of salt from Salar de Uyuni daily. What is the amount of salt that Billy has after 2 days?

50. The biggest carnival in the world, the Rio carnival in Brazil, starts at 12 PM and ends at 4 PM. How many hours was the carnival in total?

Going well so far and having fun? Keep guessing, my dear friends!

51. A church in Colombia has this pattern on the wall. It is 5, 10, 15 and 20. Can you tell the next number in the pattern?

52. The Perito Moreno glacier in Argentina is growing 8 inches every year. After two years, how much will it have grown?

53. The liquid rainbow river in Colombia has 10 colorful rocks in it. Every rock has 2 holes. What is the total number of holes?

54. The shape of a roundabout in Uruguay does not have any vertices. Can you guess the shape?

55. Guess the number of fish in the Amazon River. The answer is an odd number. That number is greater than 16 but less than 19. What is the number of fish?

56. Linda goes to the library at 5 pm and comes back at 7 pm in Suriname. How much time did she spend in the library?

57. Fifty people speak Portuguese in Brazil and 30 people speak Latin. How many more people speak Portuguese than Latin?

58. The Caribbean Netherlands has 47 coconut trees. They cut down 10 trees. How many coconut trees are left behind?

59. Gary brought 5 more shirts than Adam while going on a visit to Guyana. Adam brought 22 shirts. How many shirts did Gary bring?

60. There are 17 Gas stations in Venezuela. Stephen built 7 more stations there. How many Gas stations are there now?

61. The Amazon basin has 20 monkeys, 7 rabbits, and 1 Giraffe. How many animals are there altogether?

62. Jenny climbed 10 KMs on the Andes Mountain Range in one day. How much did she climb in 4 days?

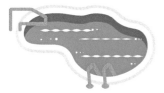

63. The second-largest swimming pool in the world is in Chile. Suppose it takes 4 days to fill half of it. How many days will be needed to fill it completely?

64. There were 16 kids at a party in Peru. Seven ate ice cream, and the rest ate the cake. How many kids ate the cake?

65. Some people went to the Machu Pichu temple in Peru. 7 people stayed there while 10 came back. What is the number of people who went there?

66. Joe decorated the Rio carnival in Brazil with 24 blue balloons and 10 golden balloons. How many balloons did he use in total?

67. What is the place value of 9 in the number 97?

68. How much time is in a quarter of an hour?

Here comes an end to the easy-level math riddles in South America.

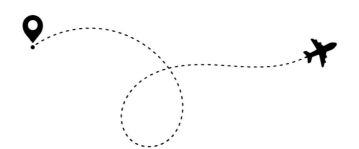

ANSWERS TO CHAPTER 2

QUESTIONS 35-68

35. 13 people did the Samba at the party.
36. There were 9 frogs in the beginning.
37. It has 4 corners.
38. Harry went to the Gym for 14 days. As there are seven days in a week, so 7 plus 7 equals 14.
39. There are 15 students in both classes.
40. The second waterfall is 8 meters high because10 minus 2 is 8.
41. They stay in school for 2 hours.
42. The girls had 30 juice boxes altogether. Three times 10 is 30.
43. She has 23 marbles.
44. The second mountain is 10 KM higher than the first one.
45. Brazil has 15KMs of the area of falls. Half of 30 is 15.
46. 5 more birds flew up to the tree to join their friends in Chile.
47. I saw 12 legs because there were 8 legs for 2 cats and 4 legs for the dog, which equals12 legs altogether.
48. It is rectangular.
49. Billy will have 18 grams of salt since 9 plus 9 is 18.
50. It went on for 4 hours.
51. It is 25. The numbers are going on in a pattern of 5.
52. It would have grown 16 inches after 3 years.
53. The total number of holes is 20.
54. It is round in shape. I gave you the hint of a roundabout.
55. Its number 17
56. She spent 2 hours in the library.
57. 20 more people are Portuguese speaking than Latin.
58. There are 37 coconut trees left.
59. Gary brought 27 shirts.
60. There are 24 gas stations in Venezuela now.
61. There are 28 animals.
62. She climbed 40 KMs.
63. It will take 8 days to fill it to the top.
64. 9 kids ate the cake. You have to minus 7 kids who ate ice cream out of the total 16 kids.
65. 17 people went to Machu Pichu.
66. He used 34 balloons.
67. 90
68. 15 minutes

CH3: EUROPE!

So, let's move forward and explore the amazing continent of Europe with its historic and breathtaking sights with some intermediate-level riddles.

Europe is the sixth largest continent in size but has the third-largest population. It is home to different civilizations, and it consists of 50 countries.

There are 200 different languages spoken in Europe. It is bordered by the Arctic Ocean and the Atlantic Ocean. It's time to investigate some bigger numbers and new concepts.

Come on, let's begin!

69. Peter bought 16 swords and 12 knives from the Colosseum in Rome. How many things did he buy in all?

70. Leena visits Eiffel Tower in France, and she has 6 baguettes. She eats 4 baguettes. How many baguettes are left?

71. Stella buys 2 boxes of chocolates from the Tower of London in the UK. Each box has 2 chocolates. How many chocolates are there in total?

72. Joshua saw seven art shows at Alhambra in Spain. He didn't like 2 of them. Guess how many art shows did Joshua like?

73. I learned a unique number at the Acropolis in Greece. If you multiply this number with any number. The answer will always be the same. Which number is this?

74. Lena visited St. Peters Basilica in Vatican City, the smallest country in the world. If she started walking at 12:00 pm and stopped at 4:00 PM. How many hours did she walk?

75. Mr. Sandy lives in the valleys of Switzerland. He has 5 sons. Every son has 1 sister. How many children does Mr. Sandy have?

76. I took 17 juice boxes to the Leaning Tower of Pisa in Italy. I drank 3 juice boxes. How many juice boxes were left?

77. The Prague Castle in the Czech Republic has 12 gates. If 7 gates are sealed, how many gates would be open?

78. There is a house in Malta that has three corners. What is the shape of the house?

79. There are three dolls in Iceland. One is 25cm tall, the second is 15 cm tall, and the third is 30 cm tall. Which doll is the shortest?

80. Two fourths of the students in Kyle's class belong to Monaco. If there are 4 students, what is the number of students who belong to Monaco?

81. Zara ate 2 slices out of the four slices of a pizza in the Netherlands. What fraction of the pizza did Zara eat?

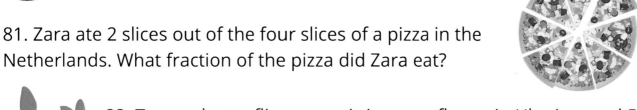

82. Twenty butterflies were sitting on a flower in Ukraine, and 5 of them flew away. What is the number of butterflies that are sitting on the flower?

83. There are 4 roads in Bosnia. Suppose road A equals 10 km, road B equals 20 km; road C equals 30 km. By following the number pattern, what is the length of road D?

84. One hot dog in Ireland costs $2. If you buy 5 hotdogs, what would be the total cost?

85. A car in Finland is 7 meters long, and a ship is 9 meters long. What is the total length of the car and ship altogether?

86. Peter runs a track of 15 km to the national park in Denmark. If he runs the same track on his way back, then how long did Peter run today?

87. A helicopter flies 23 km in Albania. The second helicopter flies 8km more than the first one. How much did the second helicopter fly?

88. A truck carries 37 liters of Ice cream in Belgium, and it gives 6 liters to a store. How much is ice cream left in the truck?

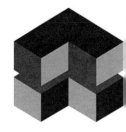

89. I saw a shape in Austria. It was a 3D shape, and it had no sides and no corners. Can you tell me what 3D shape I saw?

90. If you divide 100 in half, the answer is the number of cities in Croatia. What is that number?

91. Some numbers were written on a roadside in Denmark. Can you tell the next two numbers in the pattern? The pattern is 2, 4, 6, __ and ___?

92. The smallest town in the World is Hum in Croatia. Only 30 people live there. If five more people move out of the town, then what is the remaining number of people?

93. It snows 43 feet in Serbia on Monday. On Tuesday, it snows 2 feet more than Monday. How much did it snow on Tuesday?

94. Four people brought five flowers with them to the royal castle in Poland. What is the total number of flowers?

95. The sun sets at 6 pm in Norway. After 12 hours, will you see the sunset again?

96. Seven girls share 70 candies in Slovakia. If we divide the candies equally among them, how many candies will each girl get?

97. Ellen goes to Poca beach for 1 hour daily in Portugal. After a week, what is the number of hours he spent at the beach?

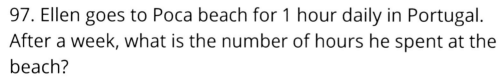

98. There are 37 girls and 32 boys on a school bus in Belarus. How many are more girls there on the bus than the boys?

99. The Red Square in Russia is divided into 4 parts. If three parts are full of people and the fourth part is empty, what will be the fraction of the square?

100. The La Sagrada Familia in Spain has 20 visitors each day. What is the total number of visitors after 3 days?

101. Four friends live in Romania. Every friend has 5 bicycles. How many bicycles did they have altogether?

102. How many years are there in 24 months?

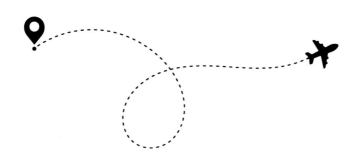

ANSWERS TO CHAPTER 3
QUESTIONS 69-102

69. He bought 28 things.
70. Two Baguettes are left.
71. There are 4 chocolates.
72. Joshua liked 5 shows.
73. This number is zero. Zero is the answer to any number multiplied by zero.
74. Lena walked for 4 hours
75. Mr Sandy has 6 children. Each son has the same sister. He has 5 sons and 1 daughter.
76. 14 juice boxes were left.
77. 5 gates would be open.
78. The shape of the house is a triangle.
79. The second doll is the shortest.
80. 2 students belong to Monaco.
81. Zara ate ½ (1 by 2) of the pizza
82. 15 butterflies were sitting on the flower.
83. Road D is equal to 40 km.
84. It would cost $10
85. They are 16 meters long altogether.
86. Peter ran 30km today.
87. It flies 31 km.
88. 31 litres of ice cream is left in the truck.
89. It's a sphere.
90. Croatia has 50 cities
91. 8 and 10
92. Only 25 people will be left in the town.
93. It snowed 45 feet on Tuesday.
94. 20 flowers
95. No, the sunset will happen again after 24 hours, that is one day.
96. Each girl will get 10 candies.
97. He spent 7 hours at the beach in a week. As one week has 7 days.
98. There are 5 more girls than the boys on the bus since 37 minus 32 is equals 5.
99. ¾ (3 by 4) of the red square is taken
100. There are 60 visitors in three days.
101. They have 20 bicycles.
102. 2 Years.

CH 4: AUSTRALIA!

It's time to fly to the smallest continent on the earth, Australia, where some moderate-level fun riddles with relatively big numbers are waiting for you.

You can refer to Australia as a country or a continent as this whole continent is comprised of a single country. It is also called Oceania, or the biggest island on earth. It is surrounded by the Pacific Ocean and the Indian Ocean.

One-third of Australia is desert. So, let's have some fun in this coastal region with our intermediate-level riddles and discover new places in Australia.

Now pack your shades, sunscreen, and swimsuits and let's solve some moderate-level riddles in the amazing natural places and islands of Australia.

103. The Murray River runs at a speed of 23 miles per second. If it speeds up with 12 miles per second more, what is the final speed of the river?

104. There are 6 kangaroos at kangaroo island Wildlife Park. Five more kangaroos were brought on Monday and 3 more on Saturday. What is the total number of kangaroos in the park now?

105. A hamburger costs $3 in Brisbane. If Anna has 18$, how many hamburgers can she get?

106. Pinky bought a pitcher of juice at Marley beach. Half of the pitcher fills three mugs. What is the total number of mugs that can be filled with juice?

107. The Great Barrier Reef is the biggest coral reef system in the world. It is in shape with 4 corners and 4 sides. 2 sides are long, and two sides are short. What is the shape of this coral reef?

108. Carol bought 27 yellow beads, 10 green beads, and 1 white bead from Melbourne. What is the total number of beads?

109. A cactus is 40 feet long at the Pinnacles desert park. Another cactus is two times the height of the first cactus. How long is the second cactus?

110. Ben has a car wash station in Adelaide. He washes one car for $11. Suppose he washes 7 cars in one day. How much will he earn at the end of the day?

111. Bob hikes 51 meters of the Great Dividing Range on day 1. He hikes 11 meters on day 2. How high did he hike in total?

112. Sixty-nine people came to the gold coast for the beach holiday. Sixty people stayed there and the rest went back. How many people went back?

113. The Opera house in Sydney holds 5 shows each day, and every show has 20 people. How many people saw the show in one day?

114. Charlie wears a hat while going to the Kakadu National Park. His hat has 2 faces, 1 edge, and 1 vertex. Can you tell the shape of the hat?

115. Jim works for $9 per hour in Perth. If he worked for 10 hours a day, how much would he earn?

116. Two students went on track to the Jim Jim Falls. The track says 4, 8, and 12. Which number will come next in the pattern to find the right path?

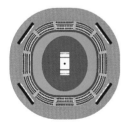

117. Leo goes to Sydney Harbor Bridge. The old steel arch is 75 feet long, and the new steel arch is 60 feet long. What is the total length of the steel arch?

118. The Eucalyptus trees in the Blue Mountains National Park cover an area of 126 square km. If the Eucalyptus trees are cut from an area of 16 square km. What is the remaining area covered with the trees?

119. The Melbourne Cricket Ground has several podiums. Guess the even number since it is a single digit. It has no starting or ending point. On one side, it appears to be a pair of glasses. What is the number?

120. Bondi Beach has 4 life-saving surf clubs. If there are 5 persons in every club. What is the total number of people in all the clubs?

121. Kelly planted 8 more plant species in Daintree National Park. Now there are 178 plant species. How many plant species were there initially before Kelly planted more?

122. Two visitors visit Fraser Island every day, which is the largest sand island in the world. How many visitors will be there in a week?

123. If you drive 122 km at the Great ocean road on day 1. On day 2, you drive for 8 km. What is the total distance that you drive for?

124. Jimmy hiked the Cradle Mountain. He started at 8 am and finished at 10 am. How long did he hike?

125. One hundred and forty jellyfish are swimming at the Cable beach. Fifteen of them swam away. How many were there in the end?

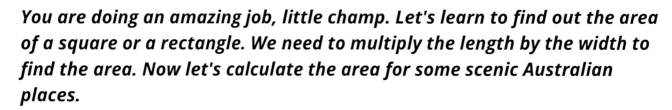

You are doing an amazing job, little champ. Let's learn to find out the area of a square or a rectangle. We need to multiply the length by the width to find the area. Now let's calculate the area for some scenic Australian places.

126. The area of a flowery patch at Uluru Rocks is 2 meters long and 3 meters wide. Find the area of the flowery patch.

127. The width of the Heide Museum of Modern Art is 5 km, and the length is 4 km. What is the total area of the museum?

128. Can you tell me the area of Hyde Park in Sydney with a length of 10 km and a width of 7 km?

129. The Collaroy Beach has a lighthouse that is 5 feet in length and 5 feet in width. Can you calculate the area of the lighthouse?

130. The Taronga Zoo is in a shape that has four equal sides. One side measures 4 Km. What is the shape and area of the zoo?

131. The tickets for Skiing at Snowy Mountains are $15 each. What is the cost of tickets for 4 people?

132. We took 5 packs of hotdogs to the Yarra Valley for a barbeque. There are 11 hotdogs in each pack. How many hotdogs in total?

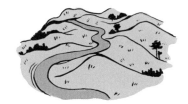

133. There are 100 paintings in the National Gallery of Victoria. They are hanged equally on 4 walls. How many paintings are there on each wall?

134. The Sky diving in Melbourne starts at 1:00 pm and finishes at 2:30 pm. What is the duration of the sky diving?

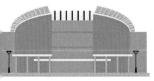

135. Bob had $87 at the Queen Street Mall in Brisbane. He gave $10 to Steve and $7 to Daniel. How many does he have left?

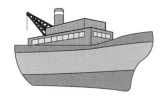

136. The ferry at the Circular Quay in Sydney leaves at 7 am and arrives back after 3 hours. At what time the ferry arrives back?

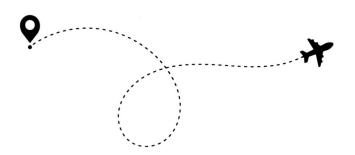

ANSWERS TO CHAPTER 4

QUESTIONS 103-136

103. It will be 35 miles per second.
104. There are 14 kangaroos now.
105. She can buy 6 hamburgers.
106. 6 mugs can be filled. Half the pitcher is equal to 3, and the other half is also 3, and you know that 3+3=6
107. The Great Barrier Reef is in the shape of a rectangle
108. Carol has 38 beads.
109. The second cactus is 80 feet long.
110. He will earn $77. To get the answer, multiply 11 with 7.
111. Bob hiked 62 meters in total.
112. Nine people went back from the gold coast.
113. One hundred people saw the show in one day.
114. The hat is in the shape of a cone.
115. He will earn $90 per day
116. Number 16
117. The Steel arch is 135 feet long.
118. 110 square km
119. Number 8
120. 20 people
121. 170 plant species were there at the start.
122. Fourteen visitors.
123. 130 Km
124. He hiked for 2 hours.
125. One hundred and twenty-five
126. The area is 6 meters. As we multiply 2 by 3 to find the area.
127. The area of the museum is 20 km
128. 70 Km
129. 25 feet
130. The zoo is square-shaped and the area is 16 km. As all four sides are the same so we will multiply 4 by 4.
131. It would cost $60
132. 55 hotdogs
133. Each wall has 25 paintings
134. 1 hour and 30 minutes
135. $60
136. 10 am.

FOR KIDS

Congratulation! You did it!

You have reached the end of this adventurous continental edition of the "*Math Riddles For Smart Kids And Their Families*" by *Maisy Miller*.

That was a lot of fun and knowledge, wasn't it? It's time to enjoy the benefits of increased family time and improved math and logical thinking skills.

Solving riddles and word problems is one of the most important skills to prepare you for real-life problems. It enables you to be a better thinker in every aspect and helps you excel in school and get better grades.

You would have seen increased and modest growth with every new continent or chapter you went through in this book.

For a further challenge, solve these math riddles again from the start and try to answer them independently and quickly in even lesser time. So you might ask, "what is the best score time to solve these questions?".

The best score time is beating your last score because learning is unique to you, and you do not need to compare yourself with anyone else!

Happy learning!

If you liked Volume 1, do not forget to get Volume 2 and challenge yourself further.

REVIEW REQUESTED

Leave us a review by scanning the QR code below as Reviews are the life of our small family-based business.

We hope you enjoyed this book as we put much effort into this book for your development.

Made in United States
North Haven, CT
12 January 2022

14712631R00020